Nature Upclose

A Hummingbird's Life

Written and Illustrated by John Himmelman

Children's Press®
A Division of Grolier Publishing

New York London Hong Kong Sydney
Danbury, Connecticut

For Aunt Ann, who bought me my very first nature books and opened the door to the world outside

Library of Congress Cataloging-in-Publication Data

Himmelman, John
    A hummingbird's life / written and illustrated by John Himmelman.
        p. cm. — (Nature upclose)
        Summary: Describes the life cycle and the feeding and migratory habits of the ruby-throated hummingbird.
    ISBN 0-516-21166-8 (lib. bdg.)   0-516-27159-8 (pbk.)
    1. Hummingbirds—Juvenile literature. 2. Hummingbirds—Life cycles—Juvenile literature. [1. Hummingbirds.] I. Title. II. Series.

QL696.A558 H56 2000
598.7'64—dc21
                                                    99-054143

Visit Children's Press® on the Internet at:
    http://publishing.grolier.com

GROLIER
PUBLISHING 1 2 3 4 5 6 7 8 9 10 R 09 08 07 06 05 04 03 02 01 00

Ruby-throated Hummingbird
Archilochus colubris

Hummingbirds are among the smallest birds in the world. They are the only birds that can fly up, down, forward, and backward. They can even hover in place.

Ruby-throated hummingbirds live in the eastern half of the United States. Metallic green feathers cover their backs, and males have a bright red throat.

In autumn, they migrate to Mexico or Central America. In the spring, they fly north to find a mate. Females usually lay two navy bean-sized eggs in a nest made of plant fibers, spider webs, and bark. These birds usually cover the outside of their nest with lichen so it is difficult for enemies to spot them.

During the summer, hummingbirds eat insects and suck nectar with their tongues. If you hang a hummingbird feeder in your yard, hummingbirds may come to feed on the sugary water inside.

In spring, a female ruby-throated hummingbird lays two eggs.

Two weeks later, young birds *hatch* from the eggs.

The female hummingbird feeds the *chicks*.

After only three weeks, the young hummingbirds are almost
full grown.

They practice flying every day.

They practice using their tongues, too.

Soon the hummingbirds make their first flight. They do not go very far.

Their mother still comes to feed them.

On a sunny summer morning, one hummingbird flies off on his own.

He spends his days catching flying ants . . .

. . . and sipping *nectar* from flowers.

At night, *katydids* sing while the hummingbird sleeps.

When the weather grows cold, the hummingbird starts his long trip south.

As the hummingbird makes his journey, he stops for a snack.

The hummingbird gets stuck in a *garden spider's* web.

The spider crawls closer, but the hummingbird breaks free just in time.

After flying for many weeks, the hummingbird reaches *Central America.*

The air is warm, and there is plenty of food to eat.

Soon, the hummingbird *molts*. His old feathers fall out and new ones grow in.

When spring arrives, the hummingbird flies north. Other birds fly north, too.

Along the way, the hungry hummingbird spots a bright, pretty flower.

But it is not a real flower! The hummingbird flies away.

Finally, the hummingbird reaches his northern home.

He finds a hummingbird feeder and takes a long drink. A female hummingbird drinks, too.

The male dances in front of the female. After the hummingbirds mate, the female will lay her eggs in a nest.

The male hummingbird spends the summer feeding. He flies south in the autumn.

When a new spring arrives, he will fly north again.

Each year, new female hummingbirds will watch his beautiful dance.

Words You Know

Central America—the narrow area of land between North and South America. It includes the countries of Guatemala, Belize, El Salvador, Honduras, Nicaragua, Costa Rica, and Panama.

chick—a young bird

garden spider—a North American spider that lives in fields and gardens and spins a web to catch its prey

hatch—to break out of an egg

katydid—a type of grasshopper that uses its wings to make a loud shrill sound

molt—to lose old feathers and grow new ones

nectar—a sugary liquid produced by plants

About the Author

John Himmelman is a naturalist who enjoys turning over dead logs, crawling through grass, kneeling over puddles, and gazing at the sky. His greatest joy is sharing these experiences with others. He has written or illustrated more than fifty books for children, including *Ibis: A True Whale Story*, *Wanted: Perfect Parents*, and *J.J. Versus the Babysitter*.

His books have received honors, such as CBC/NSTA Outstanding Science Trade Book for Children, Pick of the List, Book of the Month, JLG Selection, and the ABC Award. Some of the illustrations he has created for the Nature Upclose series were featured at an exhibit at Yale University's Peabody Museum of Natural History. John lives in Killingworth, Connecticut, with his wife, Betsy, who is an art teacher. They have two children, Jeff and Liz.